Copyright © 2025 by Lynsey Rice
All rights reserved. No portion of this book may be reproduced in
any form without the written permission from the author.

Editing & Proofreading by Lynsey Rice
Photography by Lynsey Rice, Caroline Logan, the staff at
The Climbing Hangar Plymouth & Linsey Walklin
Original Artwork by Lynsey Rice

ISBN: 978-1-3999-5611-6

PEACE OF CAKE

FOR MAMMY

THANKYOU FOR ALWAYS
TELLING ME TO GO FOR IT

CONTENTS

Introduction	9
About the recipes	13
Essential kitchen equipment	15

Muffins & Cupcakes

Rhubarb crumble	18
Date & Apple	21
Carrot & Walnut	22
Blueberry & Vanilla	26
Chocolate & Strawberry	28
Coffee & Walnut	32
Welsh Cakes	34
Scones	36
Fig & Polenta	38

Doughnuts & Buns

Doughnuts	42
Caramelised Biscuit Glaze	46
Strawberry & Hibiscus Glaze	49
Banana Cream	50
Raspberry Jam	53
Cinnamon Buns	54
Festive Buns	59

Loaves & Traybakes

Brownies	63
Banana & Peanut Butter	64
Apricot & Pumpkinseed Flapjack	67
Pear & Almond	68
Lemon & Earl Grey Tea	70
Berry & Oat Crumble	72
Bara Brith	76
Pistachio & Courgette	77
Rum & Gingerbread	80
Rocky Road	82
Date & Peanut Butter Millionaire	84
Mincemeat & Almond Crumble	87

Sponges

Coconut, Mango & Passionfruit	90
Chai Caramel Latte	94
Salted Caramel Sauce	96
Lemon & Blueberry	99
Boston Cream	100
Coconut, Lime & Cardamom	104
Chocolate & Salted Caramel	106
Hummingbird	108
Red Velvet	112
Raspberry Ripple	114
Chocolate Orange	118
Pumpkin Spiced	122

Pastries & Desserts

Chocolate Mousse Tart	126
Cherry Bakewell Tart	130
Blueberry Pie	132
Sticky Date Pudding	136
Raspberry & Peach Fools	140
Sweet Potato & White Chocolate Torte	142

Healthier Snacks

Cherry & Macadamia Protein Bars	148
Date & Tahini Flapjacks	151
Truffles	152
Peanut Butter & Raspberry Balls	155
Blueberry & Coconut Balls	156

Acknowledgements 158

INTRODUCTION

Baking has been something that has always been in my life since I was a little girl. It was how I bonded with my mam and grandmother. My family have always been good with their hands and I come from a line of cooks, blacksmiths, mechanics, gardeners and knitters! I moved from my little Welsh town to Devon over 18 years ago to study Ocean Science. And although my studies didn't lead me down the path I originally intended, those chemistry skills were not wasted!

It was in the summer of 2016 when I decided to start my own cake business and turn a passion into a living. I was brimming with excitement and began experimenting with more recipes in my small, rented flat in Plymouth. With just a regular household oven and very little counter space I look back now and wonder how I performed miracles in there. There were a lot of failures and a lot of pure delights in that kitchen. Getting a good product was my priority and that has been an ongoing process. There is always something that can be improved in a recipe. Whether that's a pinch more salt, less sugar or more caramel! Too often I find that food is made to look like a work of art, but if it doesn't taste amazing then it falls nothing short of a disappointment.

I reached out to local farmers markets and cafes and got my products out there. It was at the Royal William Yard food market that I had my first stall. Here I got to meet lots of my regular customers and get feedback on my bakes. I wasn't sure which direction the business was heading, but at the early stage I was elated to be doing something that I was passionate about and that I was my own boss.

From there, the business naturally evolved into a wholesale vegan bakery called V is for Veggies. The name originally came from the idea of sneaking vegetables into cakes. To be honest, I didn't give the name very much thought because I was more concerned about the baking side of it. And it is a bit of a mouthful to say out loud, pardon the pun!

We were in the middle of a grey and wintery lockdown when I had the idea of compiling all my recipes. After many years of baking, I wanted to collect all the ideas I'd gathered and tweaked over the years into one book. Some of the cakes are ones I make weekly for the cafes I supply, and some are exclusive to this book. My wonderful mother has handed down many recipes to me and others have been inspired by my travels and people I've met along the way.

Lynsey x

ABOUT THE RECIPES

The recipes in this book can easily be made at home with the right ingredients and equipment. I use a range of baking tins of differing shapes and sizes, but I specify what you will need in each recipe. For a full list of essential items see page 15.

Dairy or animal products are never used. I use nuts regularly, but in many of the recipes where it's possible to omit them I will specify them as an optional addition. Soy milk is a commonly used product throughout as in my experience it yields the best result. Alternatives can be used such as oat and almond milk, but the results will vary from my original. As a rough guide, I suggest adding a teaspoon of xanthum gum to a batter recipe if you choose to substitute soy milk with other plant milks. This will help to bind the ingredients together and prevent the final sponge being overly crumbly.

A small note on buttercream. I always use an unsalted block butter, not margerine, to make my buttercream. And I always take it out of the fridge to come to room temperature before beating it in a stand mixer.

In my experience, every oven is different. Just make sure that you use an oven with a fan to ensure even cooking and bake on the centre shelf. I always check the sponges by inserting a skewer to make sure they're baked through. Nobody wants to eat raw batter!

I want you to think of this book as a good starting point for your vegan baking. The flavours I use in my recipes are tried and tested. However, these are not limitations. If you keep the quantities the same, you can freely swap fruits, spices and nuts for whatever you have in your cupboard. This is with the exception of bananas as they act as an egg replacement in certain recipes. Ultimately, I want to show you the variety of sweet treats you can make from plants and maybe even convince those who make and love traditional dairy cakes that anything is possible with a little alchemy and witchcraft.

ESSENTIAL KITCHEN EQUIPMENT

Digital Scales
An absolute must. You'll see in my recipes that the liquids are all in grams rather than millilitres. Some of the quantities are small so it would be difficult to accurately measure them using a measuring jug. So use your scales to weigh the dry and wet ingredients.

Food Processor
A lot of the recipes rely on a food processor for blending fruits, caramels and chopping nuts. It doesn't have to be expensive and high end. Most household ones work just as well as the catering brands.

Stand Mixer
Essential for making buttercream, whisking cream and making light work of kneading dough. In my experience, the paddles and whisks on cheaper mixers don't scrape the insides of the bowl very well. So it would be a good investment to choose a high quality mixer.

Baking Tins
The common tin sizes I use are 9 inch springform round tins, a 9.5 x 13.5 inch rectangular tray, a small loaf tin and a 12 hole muffin tin. If you have these you can make majority of the recipes in the book.

Turntable
Although not essential, it definitely gives you a smooth finish on round cakes. I recommend a stainless steel turntable with a smooth rotation.

Piping Bags & Nozzles
For decorating cupcakes and adding finishing touches to bigger cakes.

Digital Thermometer
For making caramel and heating oil for frying doughnuts.

Angled Palette Knife
For spreading buttercreams, ganache and sauces over your sponges.

MUFFINS & CUPCAKES

RHUBARB CRUMBLE MUFFINS

Makes 12

Dry ingredients
370g self raising flour
210g caster sugar
1 tsp bicarbonate of soda
1 tbsp ground ginger

Wet ingredients
260g vanilla soya yoghurt
90g soy milk
125g vegetable oil
1 tbsp vanilla extract
1 tbsp cider vinegar

Filling
280g rhubarb, chopped

Crumble topping
60g unsalted butter
65g demerara sugar
100g plain flour
25g oats

Preheat the oven to 180°C. Line a 12 hole muffin tin with large paper muffin cases.

Start by making the crumble topping. Chop the butter into cubes and place into a bowl with the demerara sugar and flour. Rub together with your fingertips until you have a breadcrumb like consistency. Mix the oats evenly through the mixture and refrigerate.

To make the batter take the dry ingredients and sieve them into a large bowl. Whisk the wet ingredients together in a separate bowl until they are combined. Then slowly mix the two with a whisk or in your stand mixer. Add the chopped rhubarb and mix again. Divide the mixture between the 12 muffin cases, and sprinkle the crumble topping evenly over the top of the batter.

Bake for 30-35 minutes or until a toothpick inserted into the muffin comes out clean. Transfer onto a wire rack to cool.

DATE & APPLE MUFFINS

These are a perfect breakfast muffin or even warmed up with custard as a dessert. The banana here acts like an egg replacement so if you don't like them don't worry, you can't taste them!

Makes 12

425g water
450g pitted & chopped dates
90g margerine
350g self-raising flour
2 tsp baking powder
225g soft brown sugar
85g peeled & finely diced apple
130g mashed banana

Preheat the oven to 180°C. Line a 12 hole muffin tin with large paper muffin cases.

Put the dates and water into a small a saucepan and bring to the boil. Simmer for 5 minutes and then stir in the margerine until melted. Leave to one side.

Sieve the flour and baking powder into a large bowl. Add the sugar, apple and banana and stir together. Then add your date and water mixture and mix thoroughly until everything is combined.

Divide the batter between the 12 muffin cases. Bake for 25-30 minutes or until a toothpick inserted into the muffin comes out clean. Transfer onto a wire rack to cool.

CARROT & WALNUT MUFFINS WITH CASHEW CREAM

Here is an absolute classic for you. You will need a muffin tin for this recipe or alternatively you can divide the mixture between two 9 inch round tins and make a layered cake instead. If nuts aren't your thing then you can leave the cashew cream out or whip up some buttercream instead.

Makes 12

Dry ingredients

530g plain flour
360g caster sugar
1 ½ tsp bicarbonate of soda
1 ½ tbsp baking powder
1 tsp salt
1 tsp ground cinnamon
½ tsp ground nutmeg
½ tsp ground clove

Wet ingredients

370g water
170g vegetable oil
1 tbsp vanilla extract

Filling

400g grated carrot
70g finely chopped walnuts

Preheat the oven to 180°C. Line a 12 hole muffin tin with large paper muffin cases. Take the dry ingredients and sieve them into a large bowl. Whisk the wet ingredients together in a separate bowl and then mix the two together with a whisk or in your stand mixer. Add the filling ingredients and mix until combined.

Divide the mixture between the 12 muffin cases.

Bake for 30-35 minutes or until a toothpick inserted into the muffin comes out clean. Transfer onto a wire rack to cool.

Cashew cream
170g cashews, soaked overnight in water
60g coconut oil
50g icing sugar

To make the cashew cream, drain the cashews and pat them dry with a clean tea towel. Add them and the remaining ingredients to a food processor. Blitz the mixture for about 5 minutes until it is nice and smooth, scraping down the sides halfway through. Transfer the cashew cream to a piping bag fitted with a round nozzle and then refrigerate it for about 30 minutes.

When the muffins are cooled, take a sharp knife and cut out a small hole on the top of the muffin about a centimetre wide and 2 centimetres deep. Then fill the hole with cashew cream and pipe a little extra on the top for decoration.

(Pictured on page 24)

BLUEBERRY & VANILLA CUPCAKES

No blueberries? No problem. This simple vanilla cupcake batter works with lots of different berries. If you don't have fresh then frozen berries will be fine for the filling. Just add them to the batter while they are still frozen.

Makes 12

Dry ingredients
260g self raising flour
150g caster sugar
¾ tsp bicarbonate of soda
Pinch of salt

Wet ingredients
90g vegetable oil
225g soy milk
1 tsp vanilla extract
¾ tbsp cider vinegar

Filling
60g blueberries, plus extra for decoration

Preheat the oven to 180°C. Line a 12 hole muffin tin with paper cupcake cases. Sieve the dry ingredients into a mixing bowl. Mix the wet ingredients in a separate bowl and then slowly pour into the dry ingredients and whisk until smooth and free from any lumps.

Divide half of the blueberries between the cupcake cases and then using an icecream scoop, put one scoop of batter into each case. Then divide the other half of the blueberries over the top of each cupcake.

Bake for 18 minutes or until a toothpick inserted into the cupcake comes out clean.

Buttercream
150g unsalted butter
300g icing sugar
Pinch of salt
1 tsp vanilla paste
2-3 tbsp soy milk

To make the buttercream, put the room temperature butter and a pinch of salt into a bowl. Beat in a stand mixer or with an electric hand whisk for 5 minutes. Sieve the icing sugar into the bowl and mix again until combined. Add the water or milk and vanilla into the bowl and mix again until the buttercream is smooth and pliable. Transfer to a piping bag fitted with a star nozzle. Decorate the cooled cupcakes and then top with extra blueberries and edible flowers or herbs.

(Pictured on page 25)

CHOCOLATE & STRAWBERRY CUPCAKES

These indulgent cupcakes make a really good treat for Valentine's Day, if you're into that kind of thing. Personally, I could eat them any day of the week, but that's just me.

Makes 12

Dry ingredients

160g plain flour
50g cocoa powder
200g caster sugar
1 tsp baking powder
¾ tsp bicarbonate of soda
½ tsp salt

Wet ingredients

110g vegetable oil
245g soy milk
1 tsp vanilla extract
½ tbsp cider vinegar

Buttercream

180g butter
360g icing sugar
pinch of salt
50g frozen strawberries, defrosted

Preheat the oven to 180℃. Line a 12 hole muffin tin with paper cupcake cases. Sieve the dry ingredients into a mixing bowl. Mix the wet ingredients in a separate bowl and then slowly pour into the dry ingredients and whisk until smooth and free from any lumps.

Bake for 18 minutes or until a toothpick inserted into the cupcake comes out clean.

To make the buttercream, put the room temperature butter, a pinch of salt and the defrosted strawberries into a food processor. Blitz until the strawberries are pureed and mixed into the butter. Transfer the strawberry butter into the bowl for your stand mixer and beat for 5 minutes. Sieve the icing sugar into the bowl and mix again until combined. You may need to add a tablespoon of milk to your buttercream if the mixture is too stiff. Transfer into a piping bag fitted with a round nozzle and pipe onto each of your cupcakes.

Ganache

50g dark chocolate

25g margarine

30g soy milk

Decoration

50g dark chocolate

12 strawberries

To make the ganache, place all the ingredients into a heat proof bowl over a pan of simmering water. Mix until everything is melted, combined and glossy. Leave this to cool slightly so that it thickens. Meanwhile melt 50g of dark chocolate in another heatproof bowl over a pan of simmering water.

Next, top each of your cupcakes with a teaspoon of ganache so that it drizzles over the top. Then dip a fresh strawberry into the melted dark chocolate, gently shake off any excess and then place on top of each cupcake before the ganache sets.

(Pictured on page 30)

COFFEE & WALNUT CUPCAKES

I added the melted chocolate here because it gives a bit of a tirimisu vibe, but you can absolutely leave it out and just top your cupcake with the chopped walnuts.

Makes 12

Dry ingredients
210g plain flour
200g caster sugar
1 tsp baking powder
¾ tsp bicarbonate of soda
½ tsp salt
20g chopped walnuts

Wet ingredients
110g vegetable oil
245g soy milk
1 tsp espresso powder
1 tsp vanilla extract
½ tbsp cider vinegar

Buttercream
150g butter
300g icing sugar
pinch of salt
1 tsp espresso powder
1 tsp vanilla extract

Preheat the oven to 180°C. Line a 12 hole muffin tin with paper cupcake cases. Sieve the dry ingredients, apart from the walnuts, into a mixing bowl. Mix the wet ingredients in a separate bowl and then slowly pour into the dry ingredients and whisk until smooth and free from any lumps. Add the chopped walnuts and fold through.

Bake for 18 minutes or until a toothpick inserted into the cupcake comes out clean.

To make the buttercream, put the room temperature butter, a pinch of salt, the vanilla and espresso powder into a stand mixer bowl and beat on a high speed until aerated and smooth. Sieve the icing sugar into the bowl and mix again until combined. You may need to add a tablespoon of milk to your buttercream if the mixture is too stiff. Transfer into a piping bag fitted with a round nozzle and pipe onto each of your cupcakes.

Decoration

150g dark chocolate

chopped walnuts

Melt the dark chocolate in a heatproof bowl over a pan of gently simmering water. Stir until all the chocolate is melted. Using a teaspoon, drop some melted chocolate on the top of each cupcake and then use the back of the spoon to spread it around the sides. Sprinkle some chopped walnuts over the chocolate before it sets.

(Pictured on page 31)

WELSH CAKES

I have the fondest memories of making these when I was growing up. We lived in an old farmhouse that had a woodburning stove, and we would cook our welshcakes on top and eat them warm from the griddle. All you need here is a frying pan, preferably non-stick, and they will cook perfectly.

Makes 8

220g self raising flour
pinch of salt
½ tsp ground mixed spice
110g margerine
65g caster sugar
40g sultanas
1 tbsp ground flax/chia seeds
3 tbsp water

Start by combining the ground flax or chia in a small bowl with 3 tablespoons of water. Leave to thicken while you combine the other ingredients.

Add the flour, salt, mixed spice and margerine to a large bowl. Rub the margerine with your fingertips into the dry ingredients to make a crumb. Stir in the sugar and sultanas. Add the flax and water mixture and bind the dough together.

Dust a work surface with flour and roll out your dough until it is approximately 1 cm thick. Cut out rounds using a 6 cm cutter. Re roll the trimmings. Heat your griddle or frying pan to a medium heat. Bake the cakes in batches for 4-5 minutes, turning them halfway through until golden brown on both sides. Make sure your pan isn't too hot or you will get lots of colour on the outside but they could be raw on the inside. Sprinkle them with caster sugar when you take them off the griddle and serve them warm.

SCONES

Scones are a very quick treat to make if you fancy something sweet last minute. I like mine filled with oat fraiche and strawberry jam. Yes, I know there is an ongoing dispute between Cornwall and Devon. Cream or jam first? It's your scone, so you do you.

Makes 6

350g self-rasing flour
¼ tsp salt
1 tsp baking powder
85g butter, cubed
45g caster sugar
110g soy milk

Filling
Strawberries or Jam
Oat Fraiche or Butter

Preheat the oven to 220°C. Weigh the flour, and sugar into a bowl. Add the salt and baking powder followed by the cubes of butter. Using your fingertips, rub the butter into the flour until you have a breadcrumb like texture. Add half of the soy milk and mix through the dry ingredients. Add the remaining half and mix together with your hands to form a dough.

On a floured surface, roll out your dough until it is approximately 4cm thick. Use a cookie cutter that is 7cm in diameter to cut out your scones. Form the off cuts back into a ball, re-roll and cut again until you have 6 scones. Place them on a lined baking tray. Brush the tops with a little milk and bake in the oven for 11-12 minutes.

Eat them warm or cool with the filling of your choice. They are best eaten on the same day you baked them or you can freeze them for another day.

GLUTEN FREE FIG & POLENTA

Makes 12

Dry ingredients

425g gluten free self-raising flour
100g polenta
300g caster sugar
1 ½ tsp bicarbonate of soda
icing sugar

Wet ingredients

180g vegetable oil
450g soy milk
1 ½ tbsp cider vinegar
1 tbsp vanilla extract

Filling
6 figs, halved

Preheat the oven to 180℃. Prepare two x 6 hole muffin tins. Using a square of baking parchment, spread a thin layer of vegan margarine inside each muffin hole. Then sprinkle some icing sugar into each hole so that it sticks to the margarine. Tap the tin upside down to remove any excess.

Sieve the flour, sugar and bicarbonate of soda into a bowl and whisk the polenta into the mixture. Mix the wet ingredients in a bowl and then add them to the dry ingredients and mix thoroughly.

Place each fig half into the base of each muffin hole with the cut side down. Use an icecream scoop and put 2 scoops of batter over the top of each fig.

Bake for 20 minutes or until a skewer inserted comes out clean. Leave to cool and then turn the tins upside down and gently tap to free them. Finish with a dust of icing sugar.

DOUGHNUTS & BUNS

DOUGHNUTS

Ensure you read the complete recipe before starting. There are slightly different frying temperatures and times depending on whether you're making filled doughnuts or ring doughnuts. This is to make sure that the filled doughnuts cook all the way through to the centre. Also, its important to ice the doughnuts while they're still warm out of the fryer so that the glaze and toppings stick.

Makes 12

Dry ingredients

80g caster sugar

1 tsp salt

680g plain flour

14g fast action yeast

Wet ingredients

80g margerine

2 tbsp vanilla extract

350g soy milk

Frying

Rapeseed or sunflower oil

Add the margarine, sugar, vanilla, salt and soy milk into a saucepan. Heat gently and stir to dissolve the sugar and salt. Using a temperature probe heat until it reaches 37-40°C. Take off the heat and allow the margarine to melt completely.

Weigh the flour into a bowl and mix the yeast in. Pour the wet mixture from your saucepan into the bowl with the flour and yeast. Mix thoroughly with a wooden spoon. Then tip onto a floured surface and knead for 5-10 minutes until the dough is smooth and elastic. Transfer back into the bowl, cover with a clean tea towel and leave in a warm place to rise for an hour and a half.

Once the dough has doubled in size tip it onto a floured surface and roll out with a rolling pin until the dough is a centimetre thick. Use a 3 inch round cutter to cut out circles in the dough. If you are making ring doughnuts then use a 1 inch round cutter to cut out a hole in the centre of each doughnut.

Lift each doughnut onto a lightly floured baking tray. Leave an inch or more gap between them.

Take the leftover dough, reshape it into a ball and then roll out again. Repeat the process of cutting out the doughnuts until you have 12 in total.

Cover your trays with a clean tea towel and leave to rise again for 30 – 45 minutes. Depending on the warmth of your kitchen, this second prove may take a little longer.

Pour the chosen oil for frying into a large saucepan or fryer if you have one. Heat your fryer to 180℃ for ring doughnuts or 170℃ for filled doughnuts. Or if using a large saucepan, use a temperature probe to achieve this heat. Once the oil is hot, use a dough scraper to drop the doughnuts into the oil one by one. Allow enough room and don't overcrowd them.

Continues on page 44

This will need to be done in batches. For ring doughnuts fry for 1 minute on each side. For filled doughnuts fry for 2 minutes on each side. Remove from the hot oil and place onto a tray covered in a clean absorbant cloth or disposable kitchen paper to soak up the excess oil. Leave for a minute to cool slightly so they can be handled.

Decorating ring doughnuts:
While they are still warm , dip one side into your icing, shake gently to get rid of the excess. Place onto a cooling rack and immediately top with your decoration. Repeat with the remaining doughnuts. See pages 46 - 50 for the glaze recipes.

Decorating filled doughnuts: While they are still warm, use a chopstick to make a hole through the top of the doughnut. Move the chopstick side to side to create a gap for the filling and be careful not to pierce through to the other side. Dip the side with the hole into your glaze. Shake gently to remove any excess and place onto a cool rack.

CARAMELISED BISCUIT GLAZE

Glaze ingredients
300g icing sugar
75g caramelised biscuit spread
4 ½ tbsp water

Topping
30g caramelised biscuits

Use a small bowl big enough to fit a doughnut into. Add the icing sugar, biscuit spread and water into the bowl and mix thoroughly with a spoon until smooth.

Crumble the topping biscuits over the glazed doughnut to finish.

STRAWBERRY & HIBISCUS GLAZE

Glaze ingredients

100g fresh strawberries

1 tbsp ground hibiscus

250g icing sugar

2 tbsp water

Roast the strawberries and hibiscus in a 180°C oven for 20 minutes. Then blitz them in a food processor with the icing sugar and water until smooth.

BANANA CREAM DOUGHNUTS

Vanilla glaze
300g icing sugar
½ tsp vanilla paste
3 tbsp water

Cream ingredients
375mls double cream
4 ½ tbsp banana milkshake powder
½ tsp xanthum gum

Topping
Banana chips
Salted Caramel (see page 96)

To make the glaze, mix all the ingredients in a bowl and glaze the doughnuts when they come out of the fryer. Allow them to cool.

To make the cream, add all the ingredients into a stand mixer bowl and whisk on a high speed until the cream is thick. Fill a piping bag, fitted with a round or star nozzle, with the cream and pipe into each doughnut leaving a blob on top. Drizzle with some salted caramel and place a banana chip on top of the cream. Or if you're serving them straight away, decorate with a slice of fresh banana.

RASPBERRY JAM DOUGHNUTS

Jam ingredients

500g frozen raspberries

70g caster sugar

30g cornflour

Defrost the raspberries and then pass them through a sieve to remove the seeds. You should now have approximately 340g of raspberry puree.

Add the caster sugar and cornflour to a small saucepan and gradually add the raspberry puree whilst whisking to incorporate the cornflour without any lumps. Put the pan on a medium heat and whisk until it has thickened. Pour into a bowl and put a layer of clingfilm over the surface to prevent a skin forming as it cools.

When decorating your jam doughnut you can skip the glazing step and just roll them in a little caster sugar. Leave them to cool and then fill with the raspberry jam.

CINNAMON BUNS

Makes 12

Dry ingredients
80g caster sugar
1 tsp salt
680g plain flour
14g fast action yeast

Wet ingredients
80g margarine
2tbsp vanilla extract
350mls soy milk

Filling
110g margerine
100g soft brown sugar
1 tsp cinnamon

Glaze
200g icing sugar
½ tbsp vanilla paste
2 tbsp water

Add the margarine, sugar, vanilla, salt and soy milk into a saucepan. Heat gently and stir to dissolve the sugar and salt. Using a temperature probe heat until it reaches 37-40°C. Take off the heat and allow the margarine to melt completely.

Weigh the flour into a bowl and mix the yeast in. Pour the wet mixture from your saucepan into the bowl with the flour and yeast. Mix thoroughly with a wooden spoon. Then tip onto a floured surface and knead for 5-10 minutes until the dough is smooth and elastic. Transfer back into the bowl, cover with a clean tea towel and leave in a warm place to rise for an hour and a half.

Once the dough has doubled in size tip it onto your floured surface and roll out with a rolling pin until the dough is approximately 53 x 40 cm. Mix the filling ingredients together in a bowl and then spread over the top of the dough making sure that it is distributed evenly. Start with the long side furthest away from you and begin rolling the dough inwards so that the filling is rolled up into a sausage.

Divide into 12 with a sharp knife and place them cut side up into a greaseproof lined rectangular tin (9.5 x 13.5 inches). Cover with a clean tea towel and leave to rise in a warm place. Meanwhile, preheat your oven to 160℃.

After half an hour or when the buns have doubled in size, bake in the oven for 22 minutes or until a skewer inserted into the centre comes out clean.

Make the glaze by mixing all the ingredients together in a bowl. Drizzle over the cinnamon buns when they are still warm out of the oven.

(Pictured on page 58)

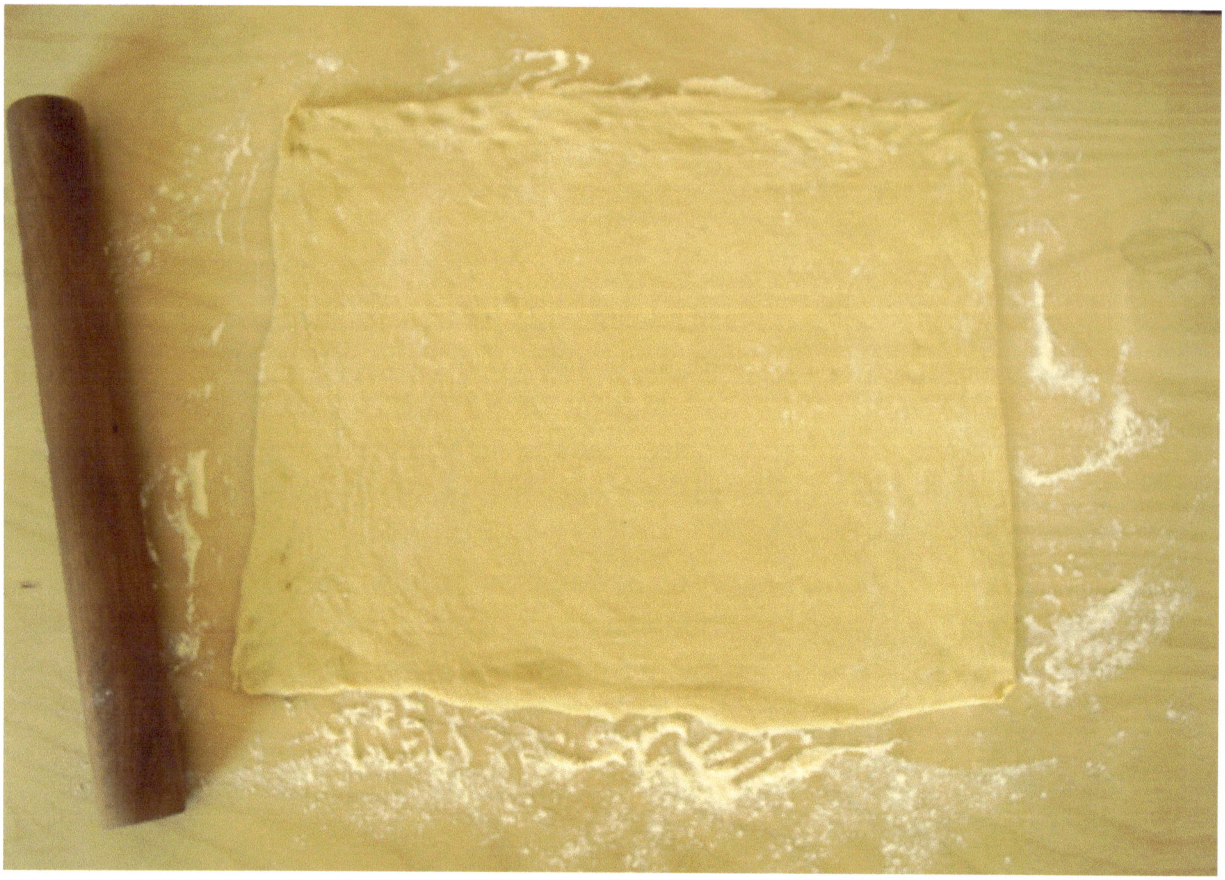

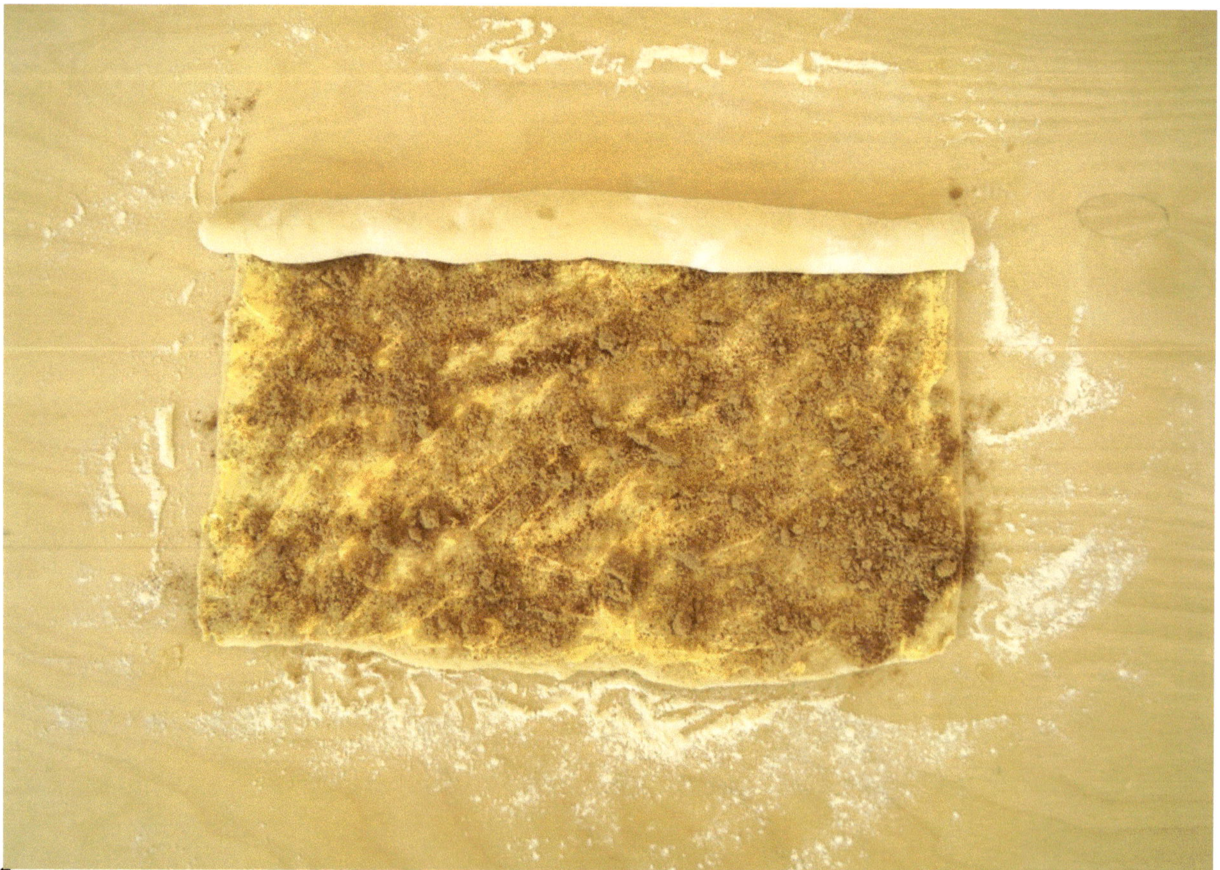

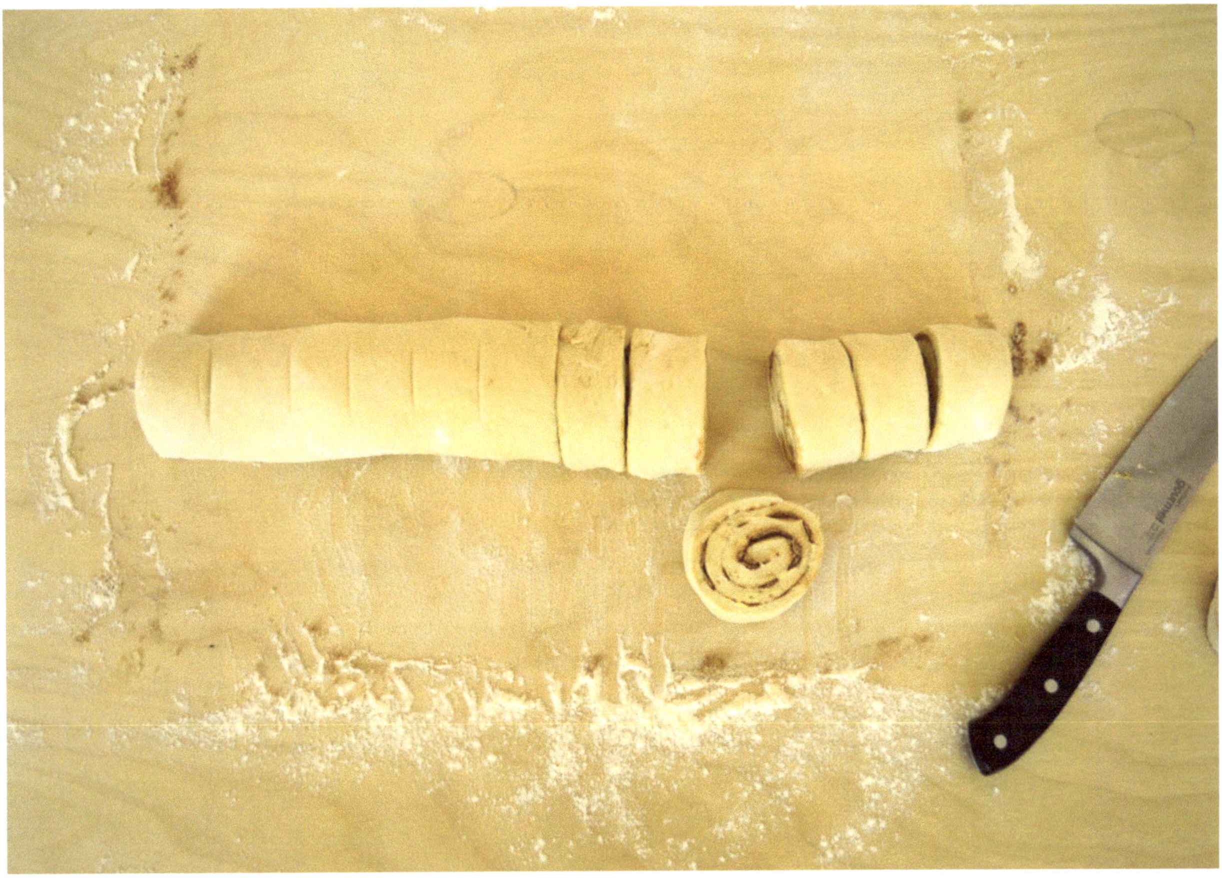

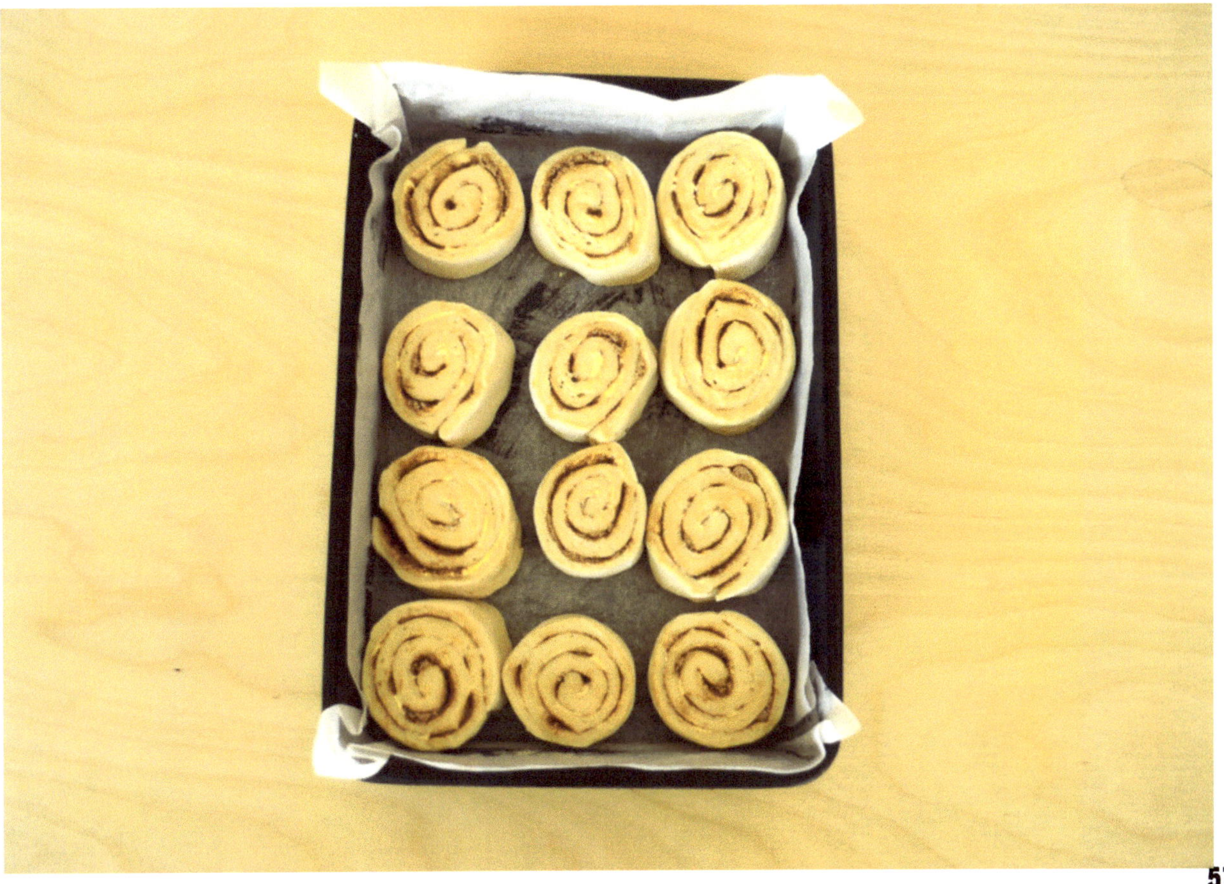

FESTIVE BUN

Filling
80g dried cranberries soaked in 2 tbsp rum for 1 hour
2 tsp mixed spice
zest of 2 oranges

Glaze
200g icing sugar
2 tbsp orange juice

Follow the recipe for the cinnamon bun. Instead of adding cinnamon, add the mixed spice and orange zest to the margerine and sugar. Spread over the dough and then scatter the soaked cranberries over the top.

Combine the orange juice and icing sugar for a glaze once they've come out of the oven.

LOAVES & TRAYBAKES

BROWNIES

Brownies were always a hugely popular seller whenever I had a stall at a food market. Something about their fudgey texture just makes them irresistable I think. The great thing about this recipe is you can substitute the wheat flour for the same amount of gluten free flour and the result is the same. I've had special requests in the past for oreo biscuit or nutty brownies, so just add a handful of your choice to the batter before baking. These will keep for a week in an airtight container.

Makes 15

Dry ingredients

675g dark chocolate, chopped
225g soft light brown sugar
75g cocoa powder
260g plain flour

Wet ingredients

150g vegetable oil
300g soy milk
1 ½ tsp vanilla paste
1 tsp brown miso paste
1 tsp espresso powder

Preheat the oven to 180℃. Line a 9.5 x 13.5 inch rectangular tin with parchment.

Add the wet ingredients to a large heatproof bowl over a pan of simmering water. Add 375g of the dark chocolate and allow it to melt with the wet ingredients. Meanwhile, sieve the flour and cocoa powder into a mixing bowl and stir in the soft light brown sugar.

When the chocolate has melted, add the dry ingredients into the bowl with all the wet ingredients. Mix thoroughly until everything is combined. Finally, fold the remaining 300g of chopped dark chocolate through the batter.

Pour into the prepared tin and bake for 22-25 minutes. Its important to not cook the brownie all the way through, it should come out of the oven with a nice crust and still a little gooey in the middle. Leave the brownie to cool completely before cutting into 15 squares.

BANANA & PEANUT BUTTER

After having this combination in a milkshake once, it's become a favourite of mine. Mainly because I'm super fussy about the ripeness of bananas that I eat. Once they've started getting black spots on them I refuse to eat them. However, at that point they become perfect for making banana cake. Win. Win.

Serves 12 - 15

Dry ingredients
450g plain flour
280g caster sugar
2 tsp bicarbonate of soda
2 tsp baking powder
4 tbsp chickpea flour

Wet ingredients
240g vegetable oil
240g water
340g mashed ripe banana

Buttercream
120g butter
30g smooth peanut butter
300g icing sugar

Decoration
Banana chips
Cocoa powder

Preheat the oven to 180℃. Line a 9.5 x 13.5 inch rectangular tin with parchment.

Sieve the dry ingredients into a large bowl. Whisk the wet ingredients together in a separate bowl until they are combined. Then slowly mix them together with a whisk or in your stand mixer. Pour into the prepared tin and bake for 30-35 minutes.

To make the buttercream, place the butter and peanut butter into a mixing bowl and beat with an electric whisk or in a stand mixer for about 7 minutes or until the mixture is smooth and creamy. Sieve half of the icing sugar into the butter mixture and beat again until combined. Then add the remaining icing sugar and 2 - 3 tablespoons of water. Beat this for a further 5 minutes until the buttercream is smooth.

Decorate the cooled cake by spreading the buttercream over the top of the sponge, add a dusting of cocoa powder and dried banana chips.

GLUTEN FREE APRICOT & PUMPKINSEED FLAPJACK

Everyone needs a good flapjack recipe in their back pocket. My wonderful mammy gave me hers and now I'm passing it onto you. One day we gave it a twist and put goji berries in and topped with melted chocolate. Both are equally delicious and will keep up to 7 days in a sealed container. If you don't need it to be gluten free just use regular oats and self-raising flour.

Makes 12-15

Dry ingredients

255g gluten-free self raising flour
570g gluten free oats
115g pumpkin seeds
115g chopped apricots
425g soft light brown sugar

Wet ingredients

115g golden syrup
425g margerine

Icing

100g icing sugar
1 tsp vanilla essence
1 tbsp water

Preheat the oven to 180°C. Line a 9.5 x 13.5 inch rectangular tin with baking parchment. Put the dry ingredients into a large bowl and mix thoroughly. Warm the wet ingredients in a saucepan over a medium heat until all the margerine has melted. Pour into the dry ingredients and mix.

Press the mixture into the tin so that it has an even surface. Bake in the oven for 25 minutes.

The flapjack will set as it cools down so don't be tempted to bake it longer if it looks gooey when you take it out of the oven.

Mix the icing ingredients together and drizzle over the cooled flapjack.

GLUTEN FREE PEAR & ALMOND

I have often found with gluten free cakes that the texture is quite dense and dry. So with the addition of ground almonds in this cake, the sponge is much lighter and dare I say it, moist! Pear is not your only option here. Anything that is in season would work really well. I've used apples and plums before as well as softer fruits like cherries and blackberries.

Serves 12

Dry ingredients
425g gluten free self-raising flour
100g ground almonds
300g caster sugar
1 ½ tsp bicarbonate of soda
1 tsp xanthum gum

Wet ingredients
180g vegetable oil
450g almond milk
1 ½ tbsp cider vinegar
1 tbsp almond essence

Filling & Topping
2 large pears (350g)
40g flaked almonds

Preheat the oven to 180℃. Line a 10 inch round tin with parchment.

Prepare the pears by peeling away the skin, cutting in half and removing the core. Then slice each half into half a centimetre strips. Keep to one side.

Sieve the flour, sugar, bicarbonate of soda and xanthum gum into a bowl and whisk the ground almonds into the mixture.

Mix the wet ingredients in a bowl and then add them to the dry ingredients and mix thoroughly.

Pour into the prepared tin. Lay the strips of pear over the top of the batter in a circle. Scatter the flaked almonds evenly over the top of the batter and then bake for 45-50 minutes.

Once the cake is cooled dust with a little icing sugar for a final decoration.

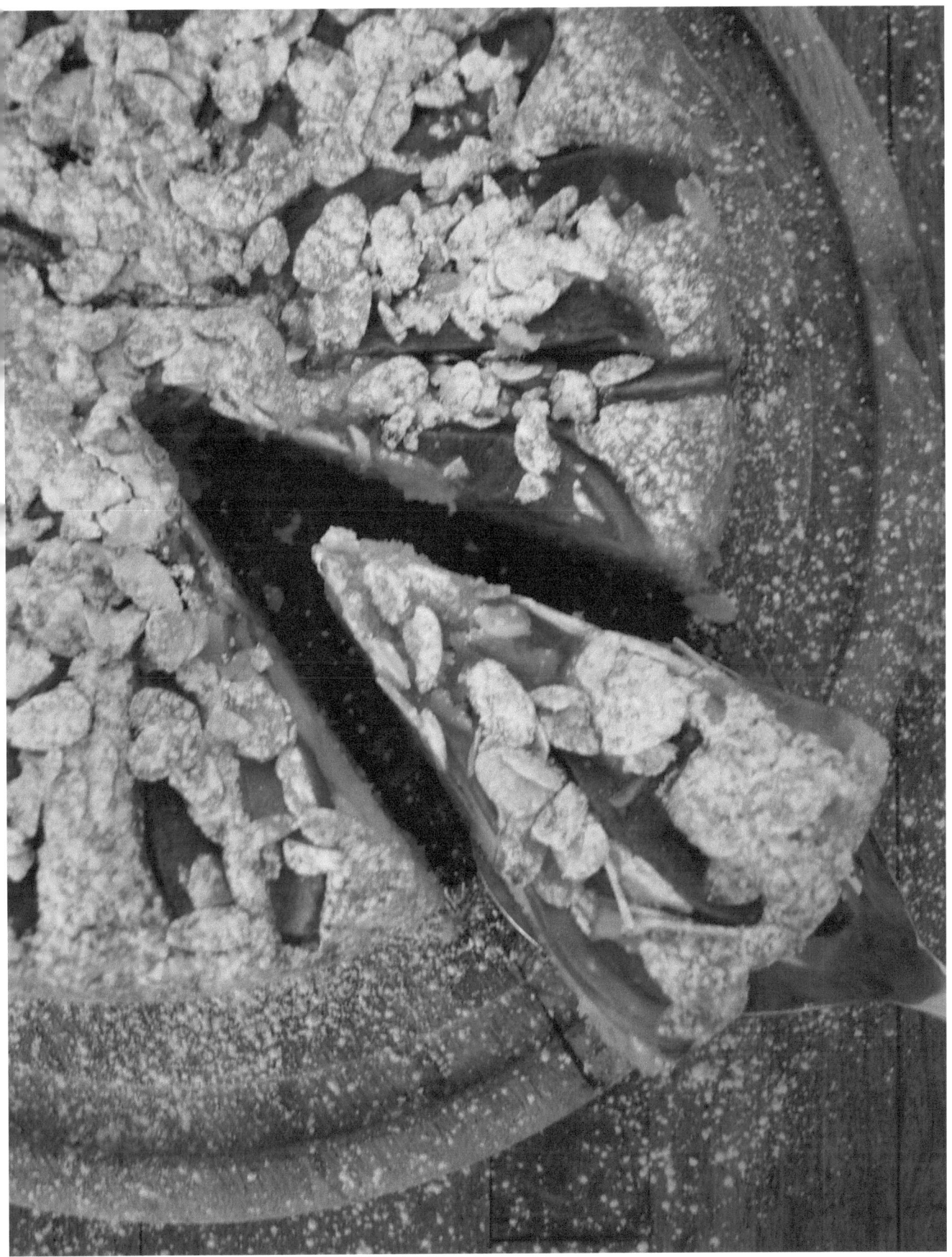

LEMON & EARL GREY TEA LOAF

I know Earl Grey isn't everyone's cup of tea, but it has a lovely freshness that goes so well with lemon. If you want to make this cake as a two layered sponge, double the quanity and divide it between two 9 inch round tins.

Serves 10-12

Dry ingredients
260g self raising flour
3/4 tsp bicarbonate of soda
1/4 tsp xanthum gum
150g caster sugar
1 tsp earl grey tea leaves
Rind of 1 lemon

Wet ingredients
50g lemon juice
90g rapeseed oil
180g plain soya yoghurt
25g hot water
1 tbsp cider vinegar

Icing & Decoration
200g icing sugar
2 tbsp lemon juice
edible cornflowers

Preheat the oven to 180°C. Line an 8.5 x 4.5 inch loaf tin with baking parchment. Add the earl grey tea and 25g of hot water to a small bowl to infuse for 5 minutes. Meanwhile, sieve the flour, bicarbonate of soda, xanthum gum and caster sugar into a large bowl.

Once the tea has infused, add it to a bowl with the lemon juice, vegetable oil, yoghurt, lemon rind and cider vinegar. Whisk them together and then slowly combine the wet with the dry ingredients. Pour into the prepared tin and bake for 35-40 minutes.

To make the icing, mix the icing sugar and lemon juice together until smooth and drizzle over the cooled cake. Top with the edible cornflowers as soon as the icing is poured over the cake otherwise the icing will set and the flowers wont stick.

BERRY & OAT CRUMBLE SLICE

Foraging food for free is a wonderful thing, especially in autumn when you can come home with bowlfuls of sweet blackberries. You can use any mixture of berries that you like here. Just chop up any large ones like strawberries into smaller pieces. These will keep in an airtight container for up to a week. Pictured on page 74.

Makes 12-15

Dry ingredients
415g self raising flour
250g demerara sugar
250g butter
1 ½ tbsp ground chia seeds
60g finely blended oats
40g jumbo oats
400g mixed berries

Decoration
Icing Sugar

Preheat the oven to 180℃. Line a 9.5 x 13.5 inch rectangular tin with baking parchment.

Mix the ground chia seeds with 4 ½ tablespoons of water in a small bowl and leave for 2 minutes to thicken.

Chop the butter into small chunks and add to a mixing bowl with the flour and demerara sugar. Rub the butter into the flour and sugar with your fingertips until the butter is combined and the mixture resembles a breadcrumb like texture. Add the chia and water mixture and mix again to combine.

Take about two thirds of the mixture and press into the prepared tin. Scatter the berries evenly over the base.

Add the jumbo oats and finely blended oats to the remaining crumble mixture and mix. Sprinkle this mixture on top of the berry layer. Bake in the oven for 35-40 minutes until the top is nice and golden. Once cooled dust the top with icing sugar.

Option:

I've used fresh berries but you could also use frozen. Defrost 500g of berries and put them into a saucepan. Keep the juices and mix 25g of cornflour into them and then add to the saucepan with the berries. Heat until the juices thicken and the fruit becomes jammy. Leave this to cool completely and then use instead of the fresh berries over the base layer.

MAM'S BARA BRITH

Roughly translated, bara brith means 'speckled bread' in Welsh. A very old and traditional recipe that is arguably another national symbol. It is believed that the cake originated by adding fruits to leftover bread dough as a sweetener. Over the years as Britain traded sugar, exotic fruits and spices from over the world, the recipe amalgamated into a blend of different cultures. This is my mam's recipe that she usually makes with eggs but I've adapted to make it a vegan version. In our house we like to have a slice with a decent smear of butter!

Serves 6

340g self raising flour
14g baking powder
¾ tsp salt
255g soft brown sugar
340g sultanas
340g water
2 teabags
1½ bananas (65g), mashed

Start by brewing 2 teabags and 340g of boiled water in a large bowl. When the tea has gone cold add the sultanas and brown sugar. Cover with clingfilm and leave this in the fridge overnight to soak.

When you are ready to bake the following day, preheat your oven to 180°C and line an 8.5 x 4.5 inch loaf tin with baking parchment.

Sieve the flour, baking powder and salt into a mixing bowl. Add the mashed banana, the soaked sultanas and all of the sugary tea. Mix thoroughly and pour the batter into the prepared tin. Bake for approximately 1 hour or until a skewer comes out clean when inserted into the centre of the loaf.

(Pictured on page 75)

PISTACHIO & COURGETTE LOAF WITH CHOCOLATE GANACHE

Courgette in a cake is amazing! It doesn't have a strong flavour but it stops the cake from drying out. See how I avoided saying the word moist? Dammit.

Serves 6

Dry ingredients

200g plain flour
65g cocoa powder
250g caster sugar
1½ tsp baking powder
¾ tsp bicarbonate of soda
1 medium courgette

Wet ingredients

100g vegetable oil
225g soy milk
2 tsp vanilla essence

Ganache

75g dark chocolate
40g margarine
50g soy milk

Preheat the oven to 180℃. Prepare an 8.5 x 4.5 inch loaf tin by using a square of baking parchment and spreading a thin layer of vegan margarine over the inside of the tin. Then sprinkle some icing sugar into the tin so that it sticks to the margarine. Tap the tin upside down to remove any excess. All the base and sides of the tin should now be coated.

Prepare your courgette by grating it into a sieve over a bowl. Then squeeze the grated courgette with your hand to remove the excess moisture. Then weigh out 200g of the courgette and put to one side.

Sieve the flour, sugar, baking powder and bicarbonate of soda into a mixing bowl. Slowly mix the wet ingredients into the bowl and combine to make a smooth batter. Add in your courgette. Pour into the loaf tin and bake for 60-65 minutes.

Continues on page 78

Decoration

Chopped pistachios (optional)

To make the ganache, place all the ingredients into a heat proof bowl over a pan of simmering water. Mix until everything is melted, combined and glossy. Leave this to cool slightly so that it thickens and then pour over the top of the cooled cake. Top with chopped pistachios.

RUM & GINGERBREAD

I love how dark and sticky this loaf is from the treacle. The syrup in the jar of stem ginger is like liquid gold so never throw it away. I like to brush the top of the cake with the ginger infused syrup because it gives the finished cake a lovely glaze and an extra punch of ginger flavour. You can also use rum flavouring if you're steering clear of the booze cupboard.

Serves 6

Dry ingredients
225g self rasing flour
1 tsp bicarbonate of soda
1 ½ tbsp ground ginger
½ tsp mixed spice
50g chopped stem ginger

Wet ingredients
115g margarine
115g treacle
115g golden syrup
230g soy milk
2 tbsp dark rum

Preheat the oven to 180℃. Prepare an 8.5 x 4.5 inch loaf tin by using a square of baking parchment and spreading a thin layer of vegan margarine over the inside of the tin. Then sprinkle some icing sugar into the tin so that it sticks to the margarine. Tap the tin upside down to remove any excess.

Start by weighing all the wet ingredients into a saucepan. Place over a gentle heat until the margarine is melted and stir to combine with the milk and syrups.

Sieve the dry ingredients into a mixing bowl and then add in the chopped stem ginger and the wet ingredients from your saucepan. Thoroughly mix together with a whisk and then pour into your loaf tin. Bake for 35 minutes until a skewer inserted into the centre of the loaf comes out clean. Brush some ginger syrup over the top when cooled.

ROCKY ROAD

This is a great recipe for using up nuts and biscuits in the back of the cupboard. For a Christmas version, adding half a teaspoon of peppermint extract works well. You could also substitute the raisins for dried cranberries.

Serves 9

125g butter
300g dark chocolate
90g golden syrup
175g crushed digestive biscuits
50g raisins
60g vegan marshmallows
50g pistachios (optional)

Topping
10g vegan marshmallows
10g pistachios (optional)

Line an 8 x 8 inch square tin with parchment.

Chop the dark chocolate into small chunks and add to a heatproof bowl with the butter and golden syrup. Heat gently over a pan of boiling water and stir until the chocolate and butter have melted and the mixture is combined.

In a separate larger bowl, add the digestive biscuits, raisins, marshmallows and pistachios. Pour in the chocolate mixture and mix thoroughly. Pour into your prepared tin and top with the extra marshmallows and pistachios.

Place your rocky road into the fridge to allow it to cool and set before cutting.

GLUTEN FREE DATE & PEANUT BUTTER MILLIONAIRE SHORTBREAD

Dates are probably my favourite ingredient as a baker. They are natures way of making something sweet and great if you want to use less refined sugar. There is a few processes to this recipe but the outcome is really worth the effort.

Serves 15

Biscuit base

125g butter
125g demerara sugar
210g gluten free self raising flour
2 tsp ground chia seeds
2 tbsp water

Date caramel

500g pitted medjool dates
150g smooth peanut butter
½ tbsp vanilla essence
60g coconut oil, melted
160g water

80g salted peanuts

Preheat the oven to 180°C. Line a 9.5 x 13.5 inch rectangular tin with baking parchment.

Mix the ground chia seeds with 2 tablespoons of water in a small bowl and leave for 2 minutes to thicken.

Chop the butter into small chunks and add to a mixing bowl with the flour and demerara sugar. Mix with your fingertips until the butter is combined and the mixture resembles a breadcrumb like texture. Add the chia and water mixture and mix again to combine. Press the mixture into the prepared tin and bake for 25 minutes.

To make the caramel, blend all the ingredients in a food processor until smooth. Spread over the cooled biscuit base and evenly scatter the peanuts over the top and press into the caramel.

Continues on page 86

Chocolate layer

300g dark chocolate

30g coconut oil

Finally, melt your dark chocolate and coconut oil together in a heat proof bowl over a small saucepan of gently simmering water. Stir them to combine, and then pour this over your caramel layer and allow to cool and set. Once the chocolate layer has hardened you can cut them into 15 squares. The easiest way to do this is to put a sharp knife into a jug of boiling water for a few minutes. Dry it with a tea towel and then gently cut through the layers. This will stop the chocolate layer cracking and give you a nice clean edge on every slice.

MINCEMEAT & ALMOND CRUMBLE SLICE

I absolutely love that Christmassy time of year when all the fruity and spiced treats start appearing. However, making individual mince pies is far too fiddly and time consuming for me. So I came up with this Crumble Slice which combines all those lovely satisfying flavours and textures. This is always a big hit with the cafes on the lead up to Christmas time. You can make it gluten free by simply swapping the flour for a gluten free self raising flour.

Serves 12 - 15

Dry ingredients
415g Self raising flour
250g demerara sugar
250g butter, cubed
1 ½ tbsp ground chia seeds
60g ground almonds
40g flaked almonds
500g mincemeat

Decoration
Icing sugar

Preheat the oven to 180°C. Line a 9.5 x 13.5 inch rectangular tin with baking parchment.

Mix the ground chia seeds with 4 ½ tablespoons of water in a small bowl and leave for 2 minutes to thicken.

Add the butter to a mixing bowl with the flour and demerara sugar. Rub the flour and sugar into the butter so that the mixture resembles a breadcrumb like texture. Add the chia and water mixture and mix again to combine. Take about two thirds of the mixture and press into the prepared tin. Spread the mincemeat evenly on top.

Add the flaked and ground almonds to the remaining crumble mixture and mix. Gently scatter this mixture on top of the mincemeat layer. Bake in the oven for 35-40 minutes until the top is nice and golden.

Once cooled dust the top with icing sugar.

SPONGES

COCONUT, MANGO & PASSIONFRUIT

This cake reminds me of my friends wedding where cocktails were flowing on arrival. This is like a pornstar martini but in cake form. If you can't find fresh passionfruit use a ready prepared puree or coulis. These are available at most larger supermarkets.

Serves 12

Dry ingredients

425g self raising flour

100g desiccated coconut

300g caster sugar

1 ½ tsp bicarbonate of soda

1 tsp xanthum gum

Wet ingredients

180g vegetable oil

400g coconut milk

50g water

1 ½ tbsp cider vinegar

Preheat the oven to 180°C. Line two 9 inch round tins with baking parchment. Take the dry ingredients apart from the coconut and sieve them into a large bowl. Whisk the wet ingredients together in a separate bowl until they are combined. Then slowly combine the two with a whisk or in your stand mixer. Add the coconut and mix thoroughly.

Pour into the prepared tin and bake for 30-35 minutes.

To make the icing, melt the creamed coconut by placing the sachet into a bowl and cover with hot water. Once melted weigh out 50g and add it to a mixing bowl with the butter. Beat in a stand mixer or with an electric hand whisk for 5 minutes. Sieve the icing sugar into the bowl and mix again until combined.

Buttercream

400g icing sugar

150g butter

50g creamed coconut

2-3 tbsp water

Decoration

Mango

Passionfruit

Flaked coconut

Add the water into the bowl and mix again until the buttercream is smooth and pliable.

Decorate the cooled cake by adding a few spoonfuls of buttercream to sandwich the sponges together. Use the rest to completely cover the top and sides.

Decorate with slices of fresh mango, the seeds and pulp of the passionfruits, and toasted flakes of coconut.

(Pictured on page 92)

CHAI CARAMEL LATTE CAKE

This cake was one of the originals way back when V is for Veggies first started. It's just one of the many things that come from India that I've completely fallen in love with. The sweet spices take me back to sitting in a chai shop in the sunshine with street dogs strolling past. My personal slice of bliss.

Serves 12

Dry ingredients

420g plain flour
2 tsp baking powder
1 ½ tsp bicarbonate of soda
400g caster sugar
1 tsp cinnamon
1 tsp ground ginger
½ tsp ground cloves
½ tsp ground nutmeg
½ tsp ground allspice
½ tsp ground cardamom
¼ tsp ground black pepper
1 tsp salt

Wet ingredients

220g vegetable oil
490g soy milk
1 tbsp vanilla extract
1 tbsp cider vinegar

Preheat the oven to 180°C. Line two 9 inch round tins with baking parchment. Sieve the dry ingredients into a large bowl. Whisk the wet ingredients together in a separate bowl until they are combined. Then slowly mix them together with a whisk or in your stand mixer.

Pour into the prepared tin and bake for 30-35 minutes.

To make the icing, put the room temperature butter and a pinch of salt into a bowl. Beat in a stand mixer or with an electric hand whisk for 5 minutes. Sieve the icing sugar into the bowl and mix again until combined. Add the water or milk and vanilla into the bowl and mix again until the buttercream is smooth and pliable.

Decorate the cooled cake by adding a few spoonfuls of buttercream to sandwich the sponges together. Use the rest to completely cover the top and sides.

Buttercream
400g icing sugar
200g butter
pinch of salt
1 tsp vanilla paste
3 tbsp soy milk

Decoration
Cinnamon sticks
Star anise
Caramel sauce (page 96)

Drizzle the caramel sauce over the top and decorate with cinnamon sticks and star anise.

(Pictured on page 93)

SALTED CARAMEL SAUCE

Be super careful when making this recipe. The sugar can burn very easily if left unattended so try not to take your eyes off it. Boiling sugar is also ferociously hot so be aware that it might spit when adding the coconut milk to it.

150g caster sugar
200g coconut milk
11g liquid glucose
¼ tsp salt
15g cornflour
50g butter

To make the caramel, put the caster sugar into a saucepan on a medium heat to melt and turn golden brown. Don't stir the sugar or it will crystallise. Instead, tilt and swirl the pan over the heat.

Meanwhile, heat the coconut milk, liquid glucose and salt in a separate saucepan to 80℃. Take off the heat and leave to cool slightly. Weigh the cornflour into a small bowl and whisk the coconut milk mixture into it. When your sugar has completely melted, pour your coconut milk mixture into the hot sugar followed by the butter. Whisk until the butter has melted and everything is combined.

Pour the caramel sauce into a small bowl and cover the surface with cling film to prevent a skin forming.

After it has cooled, use a stick blender to make the sauce completely smooth. Alternatively you could pour the sauce into a blender or food processor. Then transfer it into a jar or sealed container and keep in the fridge for up to a week.

LEMON & BLUEBERRY CAKE

Serves 12

Dry ingredients

525g self raising flour

300g caster sugar

1 ½ tsp bicarbonate of soda

1 tsp xanthum gum

Wet ingredients

180g vegetable oil

100g lemon juice

350g soy milk

1 ½ tbsp cider vinegar

zest of 2 lemons

Buttercream

400g icing sugar

200g butter

2-3 tbsp lemon juice

Decoration

100g blueberries for filling plus more to decorate

nasturtiums (optional)

Preheat the oven to 180℃. Line two 9 inch round tins with baking parchment. Take the dry ingredients and sieve them into a large bowl. Whisk the wet ingredients together in a separate bowl until they are combined. Then slowly combine the two with a whisk or in your stand mixer. Pour the mixture into the prepared tins. Scatter 100g of fresh blueberries over the surface of the batter in the two tins and bake for 25-30 minutes.

To make the icing, put the room temperature butter and a pinch of salt into a bowl. Beat in a stand mixer or with an electric hand whisk for 5 minutes. Sieve the icing sugar into the bowl and mix again until combined. Add the lemon juice and mix again for a few minutes until the buttercream is smooth.

Sandwich the cooled sponges together with half the buttercream by using a piping bag and a star nozzle. Use the other half of the buttercream to cover the top and then decorate with more blueberries and edible flowers

BOSTON CREAM CAKE

In the States they named this a Boston Cream Pie because the tins used to make cakes were also used to make pies. Anyway... all you need to know is that this light vanilla sponge is filled with cream and covered in rich chocolate. Nice.

Serves 12

Dry ingredients
525g self raising flour
1 ½ tsp bicarbonate of soda
300g caster sugar

Wet ingredients
180g vegetable oil
450g soy milk
1 tbsp vanilla extract
1 ½ tbsp cider vinegar

Whipped cream
250g double cream
50g icing sugar
2 tsp vanilla extract
¼ tsp xanthum gum

Preheat the oven to 180℃. Line two 9 inch round tins with baking parchment. Sieve the dry ingredients into a large bowl. Whisk the wet ingredients together in a separate bowl until they are combined. Then slowly mix the two with a whisk or in your stand mixer.

Pour into the prepared tin and bake for 30-35 minutes.

To make the whipped cream, add the cream, vanilla and xanthum gum to a stand mixer bowl or a large bowl if you are using a hand mixer. Whip the cream on a high setting until it is thick and aerated. This usually takes about 5 minutes. Then sieve in the icing sugar and whip again for 1-2 minutes.

Decorate the cooled cake by adding a few spoonfuls of the whipped cream to sandwich the sponges together. Use the rest to cover the top and sides. Refrigerate the cake to keep the cream cold.

Chocolate ganache

200g dark chocolate

110g margarine

130g soy milk

Decoration

Chopped almonds, optional

To make the ganache, add the ingredients to a small heatproof bowl over a pan of simmering water. Stir until the chocolate has melted and the ganache is glossy. Take the bowl off the heat and leave to cool. If you have a temperature probe, let the ganache cool to 18°C. If you don't have a probe, you are looking for your ganache to thicken and be pourable but not so cool that it has set firmly.

Remove your cake from the fridge. Here comes the messy part. Pour your ganache over the top and sides of the cake until all the cream is covered. You can put your cake on a wire rack over a large baking tray to catch the excess. You can also use a spatula to help smooth the ganache around the top and sides.

Leave the ganache to set. Then put your cake onto a large plate or serving board. Then press some chopped almonds around the base of the cake to finish.

(Pictured on page 102)

COCONUT, LIME & CARDAMOM CAKE

Serves 12

Dry ingredients
425g self raising flour
100g desiccated coconut
300g caster sugar
1 ½ tsp bicarbonate of soda
½ tsp xanthum gum
1 tsp ground cardamom

Wet ingredients
180g vegetable oil
400g coconut milk
50g lime juice
zest of two limes
1 ½ tbsp cider vinegar

Buttercream
75g butter
25g creamed coconut
200g icing sugar
1-2 tbsp lime juice

Decoration
Lime zest
Coconut flakes

Preheat the oven to 180°C. Line a 10 inch round tin with baking parchment. Take the dry ingredients, apart from the coconut, and sieve them into a large bowl. Whisk the wet ingredients together in a separate bowl until they are combined. Then slowly combine the two with a whisk or in your stand mixer. Add the coconut and mix thoroughly.

Pour into the prepared tin and bake for 35-40 minutes.

To make the icing, melt the creamed coconut by placing the sachet into a bowl and cover with hot water. Once melted weigh out 25g and add it to a mixing bowl with the butter. Beat in a stand mixer or with an electric hand whisk for 5 minutes. Sieve the icing sugar into the bowl and mix again until combined. Add the lime juice and mix again until the buttercream is smooth and pliable.

Decorate the cooled cake by spreading the icing to the top of the cake and decorate with flakes of coconut.

CHOCOLATE & SALTED CARAMEL CAKE

Serves 12

Dry ingredients
300g plain flour
120g cocoa powder
2 tsp baking powder
1 ½ tsp bicarbonate of soda
1 tsp salt
400g caster sugar

Wet ingredients
220g vegetable oil
490g soy milk
1 tbsp vanilla extract
1 tbsp cider vinegar

Buttercream
300g icing sugar
200g butter
100g cocoa powder
Pinch of salt
1 tsp vanilla paste
4 tbsp milk or water

Decoration
Salted caramel (page 96)
Grated dark chocolate

Preheat the oven to 180°C. Line two 9 inch round tins with baking parchment. Sieve the dry ingredients into a large bowl. Whisk the wet ingredients together in a separate bowl and then slowly combine the two with a whisk or in your stand mixer.

Pour into the prepared tin and bake for 28-30 minutes.

To make the icing, put the room temperature butter and a pinch of salt into a bowl. Beat in a stand mixer or with an electric hand whisk for 5 minutes. Sieve the icing sugar into the bowl and mix again until combined. Add the cocoa powder, water or milk, and vanilla into the bowl and mix again until it is smooth. If the mixture is too firm, add a little more milk or water a tablespoon at a time until it is a pliable consistency.

Decorate the cooled cake by adding a few spoonfuls of buttercream to sandwich the sponges together. Use the rest to completely cover the top and sides. Spread the salted caramel over the top of the cake and grate some dark chocolate over the top for a final flourish.

HUMMINGBIRD CAKE

Think of this as your traditional carrot cake's exotic sister. A lovely blend of spices, banana, pineapple and crunchy pecans. I've made this cake for a few very unsure people but they are totally converted after trying it.

Serves 12

Dry ingredients

500g plain flour

2 tsp baking powder

3 tsp bicarbonate of soda

400g soft brown sugar

1 tsp salt

1 tsp ground nutmeg

2 tsp ground allspice

50g chopped pecans

Wet ingredients

125g vegetable oil

130g pineapple juice

2 tbsp vanilla extract

4 tbsp cider vinegar

480g mashed banana

200g pineapple, chopped into small chunks

Preheat the oven to 180°C. Line two 9 inch round tins with baking parchment. Sieve the dry ingredients apart from the pecans into a large bowl. Mix the wet ingredients together in a separate bowl until they are combined. Then mix the wet and the dry ingredients together with a whisk or in a stand mixer. Finally, add in the chopped pecans.

Pour into the prepared tin and bake for 30-35 minutes.

To make the icing, put the room temperature butter and a pinch of salt into a bowl. Beat in a stand mixer or with an electric hand whisk for 5 minutes. Sieve the icing sugar into the bowl and mix again until combined. Add the water or milk and vanilla into the bowl and mix again until the buttercream is smooth and pliable.

Buttercream

300g icing sugar

150g butter

pinch of salt

1 tsp vanilla paste

2 tbsp water

Decoration

Flaked coconut

Banana chips

Date syrup

Decorate the cooled cake by adding half of the buttercream to sandwich the sponges together. Use the rest to cover the top. Finally top with flaked coconut and banana chips, and a drizzle of date syrup.

(Pictured on page 110)

RED VELVET CAKE

Serves 10 - 12

Dry ingredients
470g plain flour
30g cocoa powder
2 ½ tsp baking powder
2 tsp bicarbonate of soda
475g caster sugar
1 tsp salt

Wet ingredients
260g vegetable oil
580g soy milk
1 tbsp vanilla essence
1 ½ tbsp cider vinegar
1 tsp red food colour paste

Cream cheese icing
400g icing sugar
150g butter
pinch of salt
1 tsp vanilla paste
200g cream cheese

Preheat the oven to 180°C. Line three eight inch round tins with baking parchment. Sieve the dry ingredients into a large bowl. Whisk the wet ingredients together in a separate bowl until they are combined and the red food colouring paste is incorporated and free from lumps. Then slowly combine the two with a whisk or in your stand mixer.

Pour into the prepared tins and bake for 25 – 30 minutes.

To make the icing, put the room temperature butter and a pinch of salt into a bowl. Beat in a stand mixer or with an electric hand whisk for 5 minutes. Sieve the icing sugar into the bowl and mix again until combined. Add the vanilla paste and cream cheese and mix on a low speed until incorporated. Be careful not to over mix at this point or the icing will be too runny. Refrigerate the icing until you are ready to decorate.

Once the cakes are cool, use a knife to trim off the excess sponge so that you have three level cakes. Keep the sponge that you've trimmed as you'll need this for decoration.

Start to sandwich your cakes together by adding a few spoonfuls of cream cheese icing between the layers. Then use the remainder to completely cover the top and sides.

For your final decoration take the off cuts from your sponges and lightly drag a fork over them to create red velvet crumbs. Sprinkle the crumbs around the edge of the cake.

(Pictured on page 111)

RASPBERRY RIPPLE CAKE

Serves 12

Dry ingredients
420g plain flour
2 tsp baking powder
1 ½ tsp bicarbonate of soda
400g caster sugar

Wet ingredients
220g vegetable oil
490g soy milk
1 tbsp vanilla extract
1 tbsp cider vinegar
70g raspberries
1/8 tsp Red food colouring paste

Buttercream
400g icing sugar
200g butter
pinch of salt
1 tsp vanilla paste
70g raspberries

Decoration
Fresh raspberries
Dried raspberry pieces

Preheat the oven to 180°C. Line two nine inch round tins with baking parchment. Sieve the dry ingredients into a large bowl. Whisk the oil, soy milk, vanilla and vinegar together in a separate bowl until they are combined. Then slowly whisk the wet ingredients into the dry.

Pour into the prepared tins. Mash the raspberries in a small bowl using a fork and then mix in the red food colouring paste. Divide the raspberry puree between the two tins of batter by dotting little blobs over the top. Swirl it lightly through the batter using a chopstick or a spoon. Bake for 30-35 minutes.

To make the icing, put the room temperature butter, raspberries, vanilla and a pinch of salt into a bowl. Beat in a stand mixer or with an electric hand whisk for 5 minutes. Sieve the icing sugar into the bowl and mix again until the buttercream is smooth and pliable.

Decorate the cooled cake by adding a few spoonfuls of buttercream to sandwich the sponges together. Use the rest to completely cover the top and sides.

Decorate with fresh raspberries and a dusting of raspberry powder.

CHOCOLATE ORANGE BUNDT CAKE

A wonderfully moist cake from the addition of orange puree. This cake is rich with a ganache topping but my favourite part is that none of the orange is wasted. The flesh, rind and pith are all pureed and mixed into the batter which gives it a real depth of orange flavour. You can also turn this into a halloween themed cake by splitting the batter between two 9 inch round tins and decorating with orange coloured buttercream.

Serves 10 - 12

Dry ingredients
300g plain flour
150g cocoa powder
360g caster sugar
2 tsp bicarbonate of soda
1 tsp baking powder
½ tsp salt

Wet ingredients
250g vegetable oil
250g yoghurt
3 large oranges

Ganache
100g dark chocolate
55g margarine
65g soy milk

Fill a saucepan with water and bring to the boil. Add the oranges and simmer for 2 hours. Check the water level over this time to make sure it doesn't boil dry and top up with boiling water as needed. After two hours drain the oranges and leave to cool. Once cool, slice the oranges in half and remove any seeds. Take the oranges and juice and puree them in a food processor until smooth.

Preheat the oven to 180°C. Prepare the bundt tin by rubbing margarine over the inside until all the surface has a light coating. Dust plain flour over the greased surface and tap to remove any excess.

Take the dry ingredients and sieve them into a large bowl. Whisk the oil, yoghurt and 500g of the orange puree together in a separate bowl until they are combined. Mix the two together and pour into the prepared tin and bake for 50-60 minutes. Any leftover puree you can freeze for next time.

Weigh all the ganache ingredients into a heat proof bowl over a pan of simmering water. Mix until everything is melted, combined and glossy. Leave this to cool slightly so that it thickens and then pour over the top of the cooled cake. Decorate with slices of orange.

(Pictured on page 120)

PUMPKIN SPICED CAKE

Pumpkins are never around for very long it seems. So when they finally arrive I tend to grab a load, roast and puree them and freeze it in batches. That way I can make this lovely spiced cake all the way up to Christmas. I use the individual spices but you can sometimes find a ready made pumpkin spice blend. Just use a tablespoon of this instead of the spices listed.

Serves 10 - 12

Dry ingredients

450g plain flour

360g caster sugar

2 tsp bicarbonate of soda

1 tsp baking powder

½ tsp salt

2 tsp ground cinnamon

½ tsp ground ginger

¼ tsp ground nutmeg

¼ tsp ground cloves

½ tsp allspice

Wet ingredients

250g vegetable oil

250g vanilla soya yoghurt

1tbsp vanilla essence

a small pumpkin

Preheat the oven to 180°C. Cut the pumpkin into quarters and scoop out the seeds. Place on a baking tray and bake in the centre of the oven for 40 minutes. Remove from the oven and allow to cool. Drain any excess liquid off the cooked pumpkin and scoop the flesh into a food processor. Blitz until you have a smooth puree.

Line a 10 inch round tin with baking parchment and set aside.

Take the dry ingredients and sieve them into a large bowl. Whisk the oil, yoghurt, vanilla and 500g of the pumpkin puree together in a separate bowl until they are combined. Then mix the dry and wet ingredients together with a whisk or in your stand mixer. Pour into the prepared tin and bake for 50-60 minutes.

Icing
200g icing sugar
2 tbsp vanilla soya yoghurt

Decoration
Pomegranate

To make the icing, sieve the icing sugar into a bowl and add the yoghurt. Mix thoroughly to make a smooth icing and then drizzle over the top of the cooled cake. Decorate with some pomegranate seeds.

PASTRIES & DESSERTS

CHOCOLATE MOUSSE TART

Two things I love about this tart. Firstly, you don't even need an oven to make it. Secondly, it's made with mostly nuts and dried fruits but it feels really decadent when you tuck into a slice. A tin with a removable base is essential here for getting your tart out and looking neat.

Serves 12

Base
200g walnuts
350g pitted dates
2 tbsp coconut oil, melted
2 tbsp warm water
1 tsp vanilla extract

Mousse layer
300g silken tofu
100g dark chocolate
1 tsp cocoa powder
30g maple syrup
1 tsp vanilla extract
Pinch of salt

Ganache topping
100g dark chocolate
55g vegan margarine
65mls soy milk

Line the base of a 9 inch tart tin with parchment. Put the walnuts into a food processor and pulse a few times until they are chopped into very small pieces. Add the remaining ingredients and blitz until the dates are well chopped and combined with the nuts. Empty the mixture into the prepared tart tin. Using the back of a spoon, press the mixture evenly onto the base and up the side of the tin. Put the tin into the fridge to firm the base for 30 minutes.

To make the mousse layer, start by melting the dark chocolate in a small heatproof bowl over a pan of gently boiling water. When melted, use a spatula to transfer the chocolate into a food processor. Add the remaining mousse ingredients and blitz together until you have a lovely velvety mousse. Add the mousse to the base layer of the tart and spread it out evenly. Place the tart back in the fridge while you make the ganache topping.

Decoration
Chopped hazelnuts or cocoa nibs

Add the ganache topping ingredients to the same bowl you used for melting the chocolate. Put it over the gently boiling water and stir regularly until the ingredients have melted and are well combined. Spread the ganache over the mousse layer of your tart. Finally, sprinkle some chopped hazelnuts as decoration onto the ganache before it sets.

Place the tart into the fridge and allow it to set completely. Ideally this would be overnight or if you can't resist it then allow at least 3 hours.

(Pictured on page 128)

CHERRY BAKEWELL TART

Pastry
180g butter
340g plain flour
20g icing sugar
2-3 tbsp almond milk

Filling
230g cherry jam
60g plain flour
130g caster sugar
1 tsp baking powder
250g ground almonds
2 tsp cornflour
72g coconut oil, melted
100mls almond milk
1 tbsp almond extract

Icing
350g icing sugar
1 tsp almond extract
50mls almond milk

Decoration
Morello cherries

Add the butter, flour and icing sugar into a food processor and pulse until the mixture resembles breadcrumbs. With the processor still running, add in the plant milk one tablespoon at a time until the mixture comes together and forms a ball. You may not need all the milk. Wrap your pastry in clingfilm and refrigerate for 1 hour.

On a lightly floured surface, roll out the pastry until it is a few millimetres thick. Lay your pastry into a 9 inch round tin, press firmly into the sides and leave the excess overhanging. Place the pastry lined tin into the fridge to rest for 30 minutes. Meanwhile, preheat the oven to 180°C.

After 30 minutes, use a rolling pin and roll over the top of the pastry tin. This will press the pastry into the shape of tin and should leave you with a nice smooth edge around your tart by removing the excess pastry. Then use a fork and prick some holes over the base of the pastry tart. Cut a square of baking parchment large enough to cover the tart. Then fill your tart with baking beads over the parchment.

Bake in the oven for 20 minutes, then carefully remove the baking beads by holding the edges of the parchment. Put the tart back in the oven without the baking beads for another 10 minutes.

Allow the pastry to cool for 10 minutes and then spread the cherry jam over the base of the pastry.

Then make the frangipane filling.
Sieve the flour, sugar and baking powder into a bowl. Add the ground almonds and cornflour and stir to combine. Then add the melted coconut oil, almond milk and almond essence. Mix everything together thoroughly.

One spoon at a time, add the frangipane mixture over the cherry jam layer. The frangipane mixture is very thick so gently spread it evenly over the jam layer.

Put the tart into the oven for 20-25 minutes to bake the frangipane.

Mix the icing ingredients together in a bowl, and when the tart is completely cool, spread the icing evenly over the top.

If you want a traditional cherry bakewell look you can decorate with the morello cherries. Or if you prefer, flaked almonds and fresh cherries look stunning too.

(Pictured on page 129)

BLUEBERRY PIE

My best friend and I bonded over our love of the outdoors and food. It's all we talk about. One year, on my birthday, he invited me round and made me a pie with roasties and all the veg. I reciprocated a couple of months later with this blueberry pie and vanilla icecream. It must have been good, because now I'm his wife!

Serves 8

Pastry
230g unsalted butter, chopped into small cubes
430g plain flour
30g icing sugar
4-5 tbsp plant milk

Filling
400g blueberries
4 tbsp cornflour
2 tbsp caster sugar
1 tbsp vanilla

Start by making your pastry. Add the butter, flour and icing sugar into a food processor and pulse until the mixture resembles breadcrumbs. With the processor still running, add in the plant milk one tablespoon at a time until the mixture comes together and forms a ball. You may not need all the milk.

Wrap the pastry in clingfilm and refrigerate for 60 minutes.

On a lightly floured surface, roll out two thirds of the pastry into a circle large enough for a 9 inch round pie dish. Lay your pastry into the dish and press firmly into the sides. You can leave the pastry overhanging for now. Place the pie dish back into the fridge for another 30 minutes to rest. Meanwhile, preheat the oven to 180°C.

In a large bowl, mix your blueberries, cornflour, sugar and vanilla. Then add this straight onto the pastry.

With your remaining third of pastry, roll it out on your floured surface to a size of 28 x 12cm. You will need 6 strips of pastry that are 2cm wide. Using a ruler and either a knife or patterned pastry cutter, cut the pastry into 28cm long strips each 2 cm wide.

Brush the edges of the pastry tart with plant milk. Lay the pastry strips on top of the tart as pictured, so that you have 3 strips horizontally and 3 strips vertically. Firmly press the ends of the strips onto the side of the pie. You can then use a knife to trim away the excess pastry around the sides of the pie dish.

Bake in your preheated oven for 40-45 minutes. The pastry should have a nice golden colour with the blueberries bubbling away underneath. Serve a nice generous slice with a dollop of vanilla icecream or custard.

(Pictured on page 134)

STICKY DATE PUDDING WITH MISO TOFFEE SAUCE

This one is for my dad, the hardworking grafter. He loves his food but especially his puddings. If ever we're out for a walk followed by pub grub and there's sticky toffee pudding on the menu, he just can't resist it!
Serve this one warm with cream, custard or a scoop of vanilla icecream.

Serves 9

Dry ingredients

220g plain flour

200g caster sugar

½ tsp bicarbonate of soda

½ tsp baking powder

pinch of salt

½ tsp cinnamon

½ tsp ground ginger

1 tsp ground coffee

2 tsp loose earl grey tea leaves

75g pitted dates

Wet ingredients

60g vegetable oil

20g black treacle

220mls almond milk

1 tsp cider vinegar

Preheat the oven to 180℃. Line a 8 x 8 inch square tin with parchment.

Chop the dates into small pieces and place these in a saucepan with the milk, vegetable oil, treacle, coffee and tea leaves. Gently warm the saucepan until the soy milk gets hot but don't let it boil. Then leave for 10 minutes off the heat until the dates are softened. Then stir the cider vinegar into the mixture and leave to one side.

Take the dry ingredients and sieve them into a large bowl. Then whisk the date and milk mixture into the dry ingredients until combined.

Pour into the prepared tin and bake for 25-30 minutes.

Miso toffee sauce

100mls double cream

65g coconut sugar

40g butter

½ tsp white miso paste

To make the toffee sauce, place all the ingredients into a small saucepan and gently bring to the boil. Simmer for 5 minutes to allow the sauce to thicken. Serve the sauce warm and drizzled over the pudding.

(Pictured on page 138)

RASPBERRY & PEACH FOOLS

For this lovely and light summer dessert you will need four glasses. I used 300ml tumblers but anything you have at home will be fine. Try using other fruits for the mousse and topping. Rhubarb or blackberries work really well. Just make sure the rhubarb is cooked before making a mousse with it.

Makes 4

Crumble
60g butter, cubed
65g caster sugar
100g plain flour
1 tsp ground flax/chia seeds
1 tbsp water

Mousse layer
400g frozen raspberries, defrosted
180g plain cream cheese
60g caster sugar
2 tsp vanilla extract
60g soy milk
1 tsp agar powder
240g double cream

Topping
1 ripe peach

Preheat the oven to 180°C and lay a sheet of baking parchment onto a baking tray. Measure the ground flax/chia seeds into a small bowl with a tablespoon of water and leave to one side. Add the butter, sugar and flour to a bowl and rub together using your fingertips until it resembles breadcrumbs. Add the flax and water mixture and press together to make a crumble mixture. Spread the mixture evenly over your parchment lined tin and bake for 20-25 minutes. Leave to cool.

To make the mousse, place the defrosted raspberries and their juices into a fine mesh sieve over a bowl. Using a spatula, pass the raspberries through the sieve to remove the seeds. Then weigh out 240g of the raspberry puree and add it to a large bowl along with the cream cheese, sugar and vanilla. Blitz these together using a stick blender until smooth. Meanwhile, put the soy milk and agar powder into a small saucepan and heat gently. Whisk until it thickens and then combine it with your raspberry mixture.

Add the double cream to a stand mixer bowl and whisk on a high setting until the cream is nice and thick. Then add one spoonful of cream at a time to the raspberry mixture and gently fold through without overmixing.

Crush your cooled crumble into small crumbs using your hands or a food processor. Assemble your glasses by adding a couple of tablespoons of the crumble to the bottom of each glass. Then divide the mousse between them and top with the remaining crumble and fresh peach slices.

(Pictured on page 139)

SWEET POTATO & WHITE CHOCOLATE TORTE

Please don't be put off by the word "potato" in the title of a dessert. The texture and flavour is lush, as we say in Wales.

Base
280g shelled hemp seeds
154g pitted dates
1 tsp vanilla extract
½ tsp cinnamon

Filling
420g sweet potato
280g vegan white chocolate
1 tbsp vanilla extract
Pinch of salt

Line the base of a 9 inch tart tin with parchment. Put the base ingredients into a food processor. Pulse until the dates are well chopped and combined with the hemp seeds. Empty the mixture into the prepared tart tin. Using the back of a spoon, press the mixture evenly onto the base and up the side of the tin. Put the tin into the fridge to firm the base for 30 minutes.

To make the filling, peel and chop a large sweet potato into 1 cm chunks. Bring a pan of water to the boil and add 420g of the chopped sweet potato. Simmer for 10 minutes until the potato is tender. Drain and add to a food processor.

Meanwhile, melt the white chocolate by adding it to a small heatproof bowl over a pan of simmering water. Once it has all melted, add it to the food processor with the sweet potato and add the vanilla and a pinch of salt. Blitz the filling mixture until it is really smooth and then pour it into the hemp seed crust. Tap the tart case gently to spread the filling evenly and then refrigerate for 2 hours. Finish with a light dusting of ground cinnamon over the top.

HEALTHIER SNACKS

CHERRY & MACADAMIA PROTEIN BARS

Makes 16

500g pitted medjool dates
100g crunchy peanut butter
3 tbsp cocoa powder
3 tbsp vanilla or chocolate protein powder
35g macadamias
45g dried sour morello cherries

Topping
150g dark chocolate
15g coconut oil

Line an 8 x 8 inch square tin with baking parchment so that its easier to remove them later.

Weigh the dates, peanut butter, cocoa and protein powder into a food processor. Blitz together until the dates are very finely chopped. Empty the mixture into the prepared tin and press with the back of a spoon until you have an even and compact layer. Take your cherries and macadamias and spread them evenly over the top, and then press them into the date layer.

To make the topping, melt your dark chocolate and coconut oil together. You can do this in a microwave on a medium heat or in a bowl over gently boiling water. When the chocolate and coconut oil are melted and combined, pour it over the date and nut base and spread to the edges.

Put the tin into the fridge for an hour for the chocolate to harden and then slice into 16 squares.

DATE & TAHINI FLAPJACKS

Makes 16

350g pitted medjool dates
300g porridge oats
130g tahini
2tbsp date syrup
200g dark chocolate
20g coconut oil
1 tbsp sesame seeds

Line an 8 x 8 inch square tin with baking parchment.

Pulse the porridge oats in a food processor to make them finer. Then add the dates, tahini and date syrup to the oats and pulse until everything is combined and the mixture sticks together if you squeeze it between your fingers. Tip the mix into your prepared tin and press it into the tin to compact it into an even layer.

Melt your dark chocolate and coconut oil either in a microwave or in a bowl over boiling water. Pour this over the oat mix in your tin and spread out evenly. Scatter the sesame seeds over the chocolate layer and put into the fridge for an hour to set the chocolate and firm the flapjack.

After an hour, remove the flapjack from the tin and cut into sixteen squares.

TRUFFLES

Makes 12

Truffles
400g peeled sweet potato
200g dark chocolate
¼ tsp salt
1 tsp vanilla paste

Coatings
dark chocolate
white chocolate
cocoa powder

Toppings
chopped nuts
dried raspberry pieces

To make the truffles, start by boiling a saucepan of water. Cut your peeled sweet potato into small cubes and add to the boiling water. Simmer for 5-10 minutes or until the potato is soft. Drain and leave to cool.

Melt the dark chocolate in a small heatproof bowl over a pan of simmering water. When it is all melted, pour it into a food processor with the salt, vanilla, and 280g of the cooked sweet potato. Blitz until smooth and combined. Transfer the truffle mixture into a bowl and refrigerate for an hour.

After the mixture has cooled, divide it into 12 and roll into balls. Now you can get creative! Roll the balls into cocoa powder or dip into melted chocolate and then top with nuts or dried fruit. The floor is yours!

PEANUT BUTTER & RASPBERRY BALLS

These are super simple to make and using ingredients from your cupboard. If you fancy something sweet at the last minute they can be whipped up in no time. If you don't have the raspberry powder or pieces you can leave these out and roll in some cocoa instead.

Makes 8

200g pitted medjool dates
140g smooth peanut butter
4 tbsp cocoa powder
2 tbsp vanilla protein powder
2 tbsp freeze dried raspberry pieces
raspberry powder

Place the dates, peanut butter, cocoa powder, and vanilla protein powder into a bowl. If your dates are really soft you should be able to squeeze the mixture together with your hands. If not just place everything into a food processor and blitz together. Add the dried raspberry pieces and mix them in. Divide the mixture into 8 and roll into balls using your hands. Finally, put some raspberry powder into a small bowl and roll each ball around so they are completely coated.

Store them in the fridge for up to a week.

BLUEBERRY & COCONUT PROTEIN BALLS

These protein balls are not only packed with nutrient dense ingredients, but they taste delicious aswell. Store them in an airtight container in the fridge for up to 7 days.

Makes 8

100g fresh blueberries
100g desiccated coconut
50g oats
60g pitted dates
2 tbsp almond/cashew butter
2 tbsp beetroot powder

Weigh the coconut and oats into a food processor and pulse until they are ground quite finely. Then add the blueberries, dates, almond or cashew butter and the beetroot powder. Pulse together again until everything is combined.

Roll the mixture into portions about the size and shape of a golf ball. How big or small you make them is really up to you but I make 8 from this recipe.

ACKNOWLEDGMENTS

Even after years of making cakes and tweaking recipes, I completely underestimated the time and dedication it would take to turn them into a cookbook. It has been a juggling act between work, play, the pandemic and other surprises! Thanks to my wonderful and supportive family and partner Dan, who have taste tested and given feedback to my endless supply of sweet treats.

Thankyou to Jo at Yoke The Salon. Your salon was such a lovely space to photograph my bakes. Trading a cake for a haircut is the best kind of economy!

Thankyou to Caroline at Almanac Cafe. Not only did you provide me with a wonderful space to continue baking and photographing from, but you have always been an advocate for my baking and personal ventures.

FOLLOW PEACE OF CAKE

  visf0rveg

  VisforVeg

Thankyou to The Climbing Hangar, Linsey at The Shack and Power Plant Cafe for use of your lovely photos and selling my cakes.

A huge thankyou to all my lovely customers. From those of you I met at food markets, to those of you I made a wedding or birthday cake for, or brought you a care package over the Covid lockdowns.

Lastly, a big thankyou to you the reader! I never thought my knowledge and skills would extend to this kind of creative pursuit and I encourage anyone thinking about writing a book to just give it a try. You might surprise yourself like I have. Your support through this purchase will allow me to continue living a flexible life where I can enjoy the things that I'm passionate about.

Peace & Love ♡